Fran the Van

By Sascha Goddard

"Tiff, look at Fran the van!"
said Nan.
"I just picked her up!"

Tiff ran up to Nan.

"Nan, can we see
the Big Top today?" said Tiff.

"No, I have a plan for us,"
said Nan.
"We can go in Fran
to the van club."

Tiff was not a big fan of that plan, but she got in the van.

"Look at all the fab vans, Tiff!" said Nan.

Tiff did a quick scan of the vans.

They **were** fab!

"Can you see that man?"
said Nan.
"That's Stan.
He has the best van."

Fran

Tiff ran from van to van.

She was a big fan!

"I plan to jazz up Fran the van," said Nan.

"Can you help plan a fresh look, Tiff?"

"You bet I can, Nan!" said Tiff.

CHECKING FOR MEANING

1. Who owns Fran the van? *(Literal)*

2. Who owns the best van? *(Literal)*

3. How was Tiff feeling at the start of the story? How do you know? *(Inferential)*

EXTENDING VOCABULARY

Fran, van	*Fran* and *van* are rhyming words. What other words can you think of that rhyme with *Fran* and *van*?
vans	Look at the word *vans*. What does it mean? What is the base of the word? What is another word that has a similar meaning to *van*?
scan	Look at the word *scan*. What does it mean? What other words could the author have used instead of *scan*? Why do you think she chose *scan*?

MOVING BEYOND THE TEXT

1. Why do you think Nan bought Fran the van?

2. What other types of vehicles do you know? What are they used for?

3. How might Tiff and Nan jazz up Fran the van?

4. Where would you go if you owned Fran the van?

SPEED SOUNDS

| at | an | ap | et | og | ug |

| ell | ack | ash | ing |

PRACTICE WORDS

van

Nan

ran

plan

Fran

can

scan

fan

bet

man

Stan

vans

Can